T0210021

After Meeting JESUS

MARLENA LUMMIS

WESTBOW
PRESS®
A DIVISION OF THOMAS NELSON
& ZONDERVAN

WestBow Press books may be ordered through
booksellers or by contacting:

WestBow Press
A Division of Thomas Nelson & Zondervan
1663 Liberty Drive
Bloomington, IN 47403
www.westbowpress.com
1 (866) 928-1240

Scripture taken from the NEW AMERICAN STANDARD BIBLE®,
Copyright © 1960,1962,1963,1968,1971,1972,1973,1975,1977,1995 by
The Lockman Foundation. Used by permission. www.Lockman.org"

ISBN: 978-1-9736-7245-6 (sc)
ISBN: 978-1-9736-7244-9 (e)

Print information available on the last page.

WestBow Press rev. date: 08/22/2019

Contents

Introduction

In 2015, the Lord Jesus asked me to travel around the world for two years. I stood on street corners in major cities in 22 countries, and I stood with a big sign that read "MAY I PRAY FOR YOU?". It was written in the language of each of those countries. From the start, the Holy Spirit touched the lives of thousands of people. I documented some of these experiences in my first book "May I Pray For You?".

When I returned to Canada in 2017, the Lord asked me to travel across this country for one year. I prayed for people in 30 cities from coast to coast and 2 cities in northern Canada. I believe Jesus is preparing to release a new move of the Holy Spirit across this nation. Millions, not thousands, millions of people will receive a personal encounter with Jesus.

The Lord asked me to write a second book to help people establish a faith in Him. He does not want anyone to be misled by religiosity.

CHAPTER ONE

A New Beginning

Congratulations! You have met Jesus. Yes, He is God with skin on Him. The peace He has given to you will never go away. What's that? You don't know anything? No problem. You know Jesus and that is what matters. He has given you the Love from God. We call that the Holy Spirit. That Spirit will be your teacher. You can read that in the Bible: "And as for you, the anointing which you received from Him abides in you, and you have no need for anyone to teach you; but as His anointing teaches you about all things, and is true and is not a lie, and just as it has taught you, you abide in Him." {I John 2:27}. The word abide means to hold on to, or even stick to; and with us it goes even deeper. It means to remain loyal to Jesus no matter how difficult life becomes. We cling to Him until He takes us from this life and gives us a new life in Heaven.

The Bible? Oh, don't let it scare you. Think of it as a guide for you. The Holy Spirit teaches you how to love, and the Bible verifies your actions. Your life is all about love because God is love. There are no constraints on love, so there are no constraints on you. We live in complete freedom.

Is there a danger here? Of course. The danger lies with those whose actions are destructive. For instance, in my first book I asked the question, "Would we kill our own child not knowing it was a test?" There was a church going lady who murdered her two sons many years ago. When the police asked for her motive she replied that Jesus had said He would raise them from the dead. She listened to the wrong voice.

Do I have your attention? We have the privilege of hearing Jesus speak to us. He said, "My sheep hear My voice, and I know them, and they follow Me." [John 10:27]. That voice remains clear when nothing interferes with the heart and mind relationship that we have with Him. Jesus initiated this relationship and our response is in keeping it pure. The New Testament [the last part of the Bible] is meant to encourage us in our faith and deepen our love for Jesus and for each other. We call it "edifying" to help us in this relationship. It is our guide as we follow Jesus. The danger is in putting a wrong interpretation of the Bible first and using Jesus as a backup. For instance, I mentioned my Dad in my first book. He carried a 115 pound wooden cross for over 4000 miles across Canada. His purpose was to tell people how pure and how simple it is to invite Jesus into your life. My Dad had spent four years in the Bachelor of Theology program in University. A young man saw him on the road and stopped his car to talk to my Dad. He said, "I used to be a Christian but I'm out of it now. I'm drinking and partying and having a great time." My Dad said, "Good for you." Then the man asked, "So if I were to die today do you think I'd go to Heaven?" At that moment my Dad had a vision of himself throwing theology books out of the library window. At the same time he heard Jesus say, "Say yes." He said yes and had no idea as to what to say next. The man stared at him in disbelief. He said, "How can you say that?" Immediately Jesus gave His answer to my Dad: "Because you have already been forgiven; all you have to do is to turn around and see Him again." The man stood speechless for a few seconds and then returned to his car. He sat behind the wheel with his head down. The window was open and my Dad walked up to him and said, "Jesus has a plan for you." He slumped forward. His head rested on the steering wheel and tears filled his eyes. Christians had hurt him with a Bible verse. Jesus welcomed him back, just as He welcomed a dying criminal on the cross beside Him. There are two insights to recognize here, one positive and one negative. On the positive side we see the immense mercy of Jesus to forgive us only once and we remain forgiven for life. The negative is revealed in the last part of the statement: "All you have to do is to turn around and see Him again." You can't just say that you have been forgiven and ignore Him. That forgiveness is validated when you make a decision to return to Jesus.

Sadly, Christians hurting each other is a constant problem. It's crazy. Jesus told us, "This I command you, that you love one another." [John 15:17]. He wasn't referring to people in general, He was giving a directive to us who follow Him. Almost every Christian I had met as I travelled around the world had good intentions. All of them believed that they were serving Jesus. The common denominator that stood out was that they were putting their interpretation of the Bible first. They would hold on to certain verses that gave their service meaning. Their conduct and behaviour was in danger of turning into a form of legalism, as in a code of rules to follow. For example, when I was 3 years old, a pastor came to our house to talk to my parents. He asked them if I had been baptized. When my Dad said no he replied, "I am here to tell you that if she isn't baptized she's going to hell." My Dad said, "You think God would send an innocent little girl to hell because she's not baptized?" He retorted, "It's in the Word! It's in the Word!" It's a classic example of putting an incorrect teaching of the Bible first and using Jesus as a backup.

So how do we make sure that we don't go off the rails? That's easy. The New Testament is all about Jesus. It follows through with all kinds of guidelines for Christian behaviour and lifestyle. Reading and studying the Bible over and over allows you to become open to the teaching of the Holy Spirit. But you have already met Jesus and He has filled you with the Holy Spirit. That Spirit teaches you how to follow these guidelines. You will recognize what is right and what is wrong when Christians interact. Rely on that Love that God has given to you. It will show you what to follow and what to avoid. The trick is to forgive those who are wrong. Remember, Jesus wants us to love one another. Another example of how important it is to maintain unity is found in an encounter my Dad had with a particular group of Christians. They followed a verse in the Bible and believed in breathing the Holy Spirit onto each other. In fact, the sons were not to marry anyone unless the girl believed in the same thing. When the Mother asked my Dad what he thought of their belief, my Dad quietly asked Jesus how to correct them. Jesus said, "Shut up." [He doesn't mince words]. My Dad smiled and said, "Your family is very dedicated." Later, when my Dad was alone, he asked Jesus why he couldn't say anything. Jesus replied, "That family is held together by their love for Me. It is not your place to correct them. I will judge their theology." This is why we need to love every Christian who loves Jesus. This is how we show Jesus to the world.

There is one question that will come up. Does this mean we can follow any teaching of Jesus that people invent? No, there is one correct way to live for Jesus. Most churches have discipleship programs that are strikingly similar. They agree on 99% of their theology. This case is in the 1% category. The point is not to exert your authority over them. These people loved Jesus and that was all that mattered.

CHAPTER TWO

Prayer Made Easy

Prayer is the best thing about being a Christian. We get to talk to Jesus. Jesus taught us the Lord's Prayer [Matthew 6: 9-13] which is a prayer of adoration and gratitude. That prayer allows us to step into a right relationship with our Heavenly Father. That prayer came from Him. We get to pray back, and it's real easy. We just talk to Jesus, about anything. There is nothing formal about it. He's your best friend and you can talk to Him anywhere and at any time. You're actually praying when you're talking to Jesus.

Sometimes we face a difficult situation and we don't know what to pray for. Jesus has you covered. Romans 8:26 reads, "And in the same way the Spirit also helps our weakness; for we do not know how to pray as we should, but the Spirit Himself intercedes [prays]for us with groanings too deep for words." The Holy Spirit gives you the words. You will be given a language that you don't understand. We call that speaking in tongues. The Holy Spirit will speak through you to bring about a perfect result. So how does that work? Don't let anyone try to box in Jesus by telling you a magic formula. We are outside the box of Christian rules. Everyone is unique before Jesus and each will be shown a way that is unique. The secret is in the words of Jesus,

"Ask, and it shall be given to you..." [Matthew 7:7]. We simply ask.

I found that the more I learned about the truths in the Bible, and the more I applied them to my life, the more "giftings" I received. I believed God at His Word. I had faith to let the Holy Spirit guide me and I asked for the gift of interceding prayer. I spoke whatever word or words that came to my mind, and they started flowing from my heart like a waterfall. They made no sense. This is where you must swallow your pride and not listen to your mind which does not understand it. You'll think, "This is jibberish." That is the enemy trying to make you doubt so you won't do what is going to hurt him. What you speak will become your "prayer language". You will speak these and other words when you pray. These are powerful words that come directly from the Holy Spirit inside of you. God sent this language to you and you are sending it back to Jesus who will act on it. Wow! How cool is that? Do not be discouraged if it takes some time to get it. This is in God's plan which He has prepared for you. Jesus does not leave us to struggle on our own. Not only will He answer the situation, He will develop our spiritual life and encourage our faith along the way.

I use this prayer language whenever I pray for people. Because it is Spirit led, the Lord can transform hearts in a perfect way, and you open the door to the miraculous. I do not do this for myself, but for others. I have nothing to gain for myself. My joy is to see the Lord transform a life, to watch Him heal, deliver and set free many who did not even realize how bound they were, and to show love to the people who needed it most.

Allow the Holy Spirit to set you free by praying for yourself. Ask for discernment, strength, wisdom, understanding, courage, faith - ask for it all! He wants you to become a person of compassion whom He can use to set other people free. Walk in obedience to the Lord while your only goal is to do what pleases Him. In fact, your entire life's purpose is to do what is pleasing to the Lord. Learn your personal relationship with Jesus and do what He is asking you to do. It will be different from someone else. It is really that simple, and will be more rewarding than you can imagine. Maintain this simplicity with childlike faith. It is when you overthink things that trouble comes. Not everything needs to make sense. Faith means not knowing the outcome, and trust is believing when it doesn't make sense.

Earnestly seek Jesus and no one else but Him, and you will hear His voice. He will come when you go beyond the superficial and revere Him as the most amazing love of your life. Stay quiet and listen. He will speak through impressions on the heart, in visions and dreams, by His Word in the Bible, through other people and even audibly.

It is fear that holds people back from the fullness of life that God has for them. If you truly believe that Jesus is alive and that you are a child of this King, you should not be afraid. A big part of this fear is disobedience to Jesus. When you do things you should not do you become afraid because of guilt. Then you give up or justify your wrongdoing. Then you get stuck in a pit and you can't get out, unless you choose to make a change in your life and hold firm to the truth that is in Jesus. He is more willing to help you than you are willing to ask. Whatever you are holding onto, give it to Jesus. Make a simple prayer. It doesn't have to be in these exact words, but use this format in making your own prayer: Father, I praise You and I glorify You. Father I am heavy with [name of] burdens, and I give them to You. Thank you for always being there for me and I forgive [name of person].

CHAPTER THREE

Getting Unstuck

Sometimes we may face a problem that comes as a result of past behaviour or habits. It just reoccurs from time to time. Don't shrug it off and live in denial. Admit that you have a problem. Take accountability if you have caused any harm. That will be your confession before God. Then ask God to help you to change your mindset. Don't focus on anything negative. God will renew your mind as you focus on the positive. Changing your thoughts will change your words which will help to change your actions and develop your character.

Everything that is said and done comes from the heart. If your heart has been scarred and wounded like mine, you will project that onto other people. Allowing God to come in will transform you from the inside out. How do you do this? Through prayer. Just ask him to remove the junk and fill you with His love. Something happens every time we pray. The more you ask, the more integrity He releases into you. Do not let the words of someone else hold you back. I was told that I was fat, ugly and good for nothing. Those words were a lie from the enemy who used other people to say them – and I believed it for years. The truth is that we were created in the "image" of God, and therefore His child who is perfectly and wonderfully made. Unlike the rest of creation, He breathed life into us from the beginning. Reject the lies from people who don't even know Him.

As the Lord increases your integrity, He will begin to instil honesty, confidence and freedom into your heart. Help Him out. Break the patterns that are causing you this trouble. If you're hanging out with the wrong crowd, the bad influences will hold you back. God has new friends for you. If a certain situation triggers your problem, then look for another one. Don't go along with something that will cause your problem to reoccur. Avoid the bad patterns.

This behaviour is your act of faith before God. He will develop morals and ethics into your character as He breaks the bondages in your life. You will no longer live with a victim mentality. With every temptation ask for strength and courage and He will give it to you. If you slip up, don't punish yourself. You are no less valuable in the eyes of Jesus. Just let a righteous anger remain in you to do better next time. Maintain your faith to believe in every word from Jesus, and that you ARE forgiven.

One of the biggest difficulties to overcome is a lack of forgiveness. Forgiving someone who has hurt you doesn't mean that the harm that person has caused is not important. It means allowing yourself to become free from the poison of unforgiveness which will consume you. The trouble is: it's hard. We constantly hold onto that pain no matter how hard we try to forgive. It is the prayers that do it for you. Continually ask for forgiveness every day. That forgiveness will eventually seep into your heart. If you keep your heart open and receptive, the process will progress more quickly - don't harden your heart against it. Remember, something happens every time you ask.

We need to learn to be content with every situation in

which we find ourselves. Love God and trust Him to work out things so they become better for you. Not understanding what's going on doesn't mean that God is not involved in it. The Lord disciplines the ones He loves to enable them to become more like Him. Remember He loves you and will always be there for you in every situation. Trying to understand the "why" in everything robs you of your peace. I used to punish myself over and over again whenever I made a mistake. I would dwell in a mix of negative emotions until I matured in the Lord. Then Romans 8:1 came alive for me: "Therefore, there is no condemnation for those who are in Christ Jesus." Faith is trusting without knowing all the answers. He has the answers.

Be careful not to get caught into a spirit of familiarity, where you just want to stay comfortable. Jesus wants us to venture out of our comfort zone so we can exercise our faith. Staying comfortable stagnates our faith. The words "deliver us from evil" in the Lord's Prayer contains a different meaning to the Jewish people in the time of Jesus. In Hebrew it translates better as "keep our faith in You alive." It wasn't just a lack of faith that was evil, it was a stagnant faith. Faith only exists when it is active and vibrant. It compels us to trust God without knowing the outcome. God is happy when you trust Him. If you find yourself getting confused then take authority over your mind and submit it to God who is not the author of confusion. We always have a choice. Make the decision to enjoy what Jesus died for in order to give it to you. It would be tragic to have Jesus go through an execution to purchase our freedom, and for us to remain miserable, confused and all messed up inside. No, I choose to enjoy my life. If that means I have to deal with a bunch of things I don't understand, so what? My God will strengthen my character as we go through this together. I will continue to submit to Him and He will continue to sanctify my heart and renew my mind.

Don't let frustration get the better of you. Faith can turn to bitterness if you allow it to, and you'll want to give up. This can show up if we allow a love for other things to get in the way of your love for Him. He wants your full devotion, dependency and surrender to Himself. When trials and hardships come, He looks for your faithfulness and your attitude towards Him. Persevere through the trials with an openness to change. Don't remain stubborn and harden your heart. Let the Holy Spirit teach you through the gift of discernment which has been given to you. If you feel a lack in that area, or any other area, then ask for more of it. God is happy to give you more. When you pray for it, believe you are receiving it. Even if you go through an unexpected process, you will receive more because God is with you and is always for you.

CHAPTER FOUR

Walking Upright

Jesus would remind me that He is the vine and we are the branches. I realize that I am fully dependent upon the Lord. I have become so close to Him that it is natural to always speak to Him throughout the day. His work is not a burden, but a joy. He always gives you rest when you need it and keeps you busy at the right time. You must be strong, you must be courageous and you must not give up. Know that God is with you everywhere you go. Do what is required of you even though you may face hardships and trials. You must complete the task that has been entrusted to you. Walk with faith, obedience and love as you persevere through every hardship. Furthermore, endure every hardship with thanks and praise. As stellar as your commitment may be, Jesus does not want you to think that He loves you because of what you do for Him. He loves you for who you are, and you are in His family. Jesus gave His life to make us a part of God's family, and solidify that trust relationship. Both His words and His actions affirm this gift to us.

Embrace God's power to change who you are instead of working feverishly to change yourself. By trusting God, a new sort of life will be spreading through your system because now you are letting Him work at the right part of you. It's like the difference between paint, which lays on the surface, and dye which soaks through the surface. By God's power you become someone who is dyed and not painted. That dye is God-breathed and will change us internally. We don't need to look to others for motivation and direction. The painted Christian, who gains wisdom by making poor decisions and learning from them, is farther behind the one who has been given the right kind of wisdom from the start. God's wisdom gives us the ability to use the best means at the best time to accomplish the best ends. The more you get to know Him, the more you will love Him and want to change to become like Him. We were made in His likeness. We are made to be a reflection of His perfect love. He will never force His presence upon us. It is up to us to choose.

Honesty, integrity, faithfulness and self control are a big part of living for Jesus. How do we hold on to the teachings of Jesus with self control or self discipline? To train yourself to be godly you must love Jesus and do what He requires from you. Each person is different and we each have a different testimony. Each of us has been given a unique gift that has been made perfect. Do not do what everyone else is doing or what they want you to do. Believe that He is with you and He has your back in whatever you're doing. Break certain habits and lies that we have believed for a long time. Ask Jesus for more wisdom, discernment, strength, courage and boldness. Tell Him to take out the fleshy ways and to pour in His love, peace and joy. Believe you are receiving them and praise Him for it. Ask for an increase in faith, and then ask again! If we lack faith we will begin to doubt. Don't let the enemy steal your joy and the perfect plan that Jesus has for you. We all make mistakes. That is part of the "sanctification" process where God is setting us apart from the world to develop a holiness within our character. We are entitled to ask for this sanctification of the heart, and the renewal of the mind and the empowerment of the Holy Spirit. Thank Him for these gifts and remain patient during this process. Don't do anything in your own strength. God is gentle, not forceful. Resist anything that you recognize as evil, and embrace what you see as good as your gift of discernment leads you. Reading the New Testament will help you to overcome any obstacles that come before you. Look at how Jesus walked and lived, and then pray: "Lord, make me like you. Make me one with You as You are with our Father" [John 17:21]. Pray for people and don't judge them. Love them instead. Training yourself in this way is not hard. It becomes hard only if you make it hard on yourself.

Jesus said that we need to become perfect as our Heavenly Father is perfect. That word "perfect" is more accurately translated as "being made whole" or "complete". That is what Jesus does for us. Therefore we should strive to do what is good and pleasing to the Lord because we love Him that much. The "Golden Rule" says to treat people the way you would want to be treated. Go beyond that. Extend that courtesy to those who would harm you. Forgiveness is the key. Don't hold a grudge, forgive instead and let it go. It is not hard unless you make it hard. Remember what I said about the poison of unforgiveness. When you are able to forgive the person who has harmed you the most, it becomes easier to forgive the ones who were less harmful. People who are hurtful are usually hurting within themselves.

When we allow Jesus to do all these things for us, we are walking upright.

CHAPTER FIVE

Getting Together

A community has been described as a group of people who care about each other and who share common beliefs and values. The key words are group, care and share. Christians express this community with the word Church. The church is not a building. It is this group of people who care for each other and interact with each other to achieve the same goals. It's God's family. As in any family you probably won't get along with everyone because of personality differences. That doesn't matter. When you belong to a church, the same Jesus who resides in you also lives in the one who is a little annoying. Just laugh it off and don't let it get to you. The church is important. We try to meet the needs of each member. We also want to share our love for Jesus to everyone outside of the church. We can learn what kind of service we have been called to when we get together.

The first thing to do is to find a church. When you visit a church, look to see if people love each other. If you feel a sense of indifference instead of joy then look for another church. Many churches brag about their preaching. Joy trumps preaching. The second thing is not allowing yourself to be saddled with a bunch of rules to follow. They will chain up the freedom that the Lord has already given to you. Even when it comes to giving, it should be based on what God tells you to give – not what the church tells you to give. I was praying for people all over the world for years and many churches were generous and gave me money so I could continue with my journey. Jesus told me to save ten percent of that money [which is known as a tithe] and to spend it on food for the homeless or to buy things for people in need. He will tell you in your heart how much money you are to give to support the church that is supporting you. You will feel a peace when you find the right church.

The third and final area of discovery is in recognizing the type of service that God has for you. We believe that Jesus wants us to share Him with the world. Because He values every human life, we value every human life. The church calls it "outreach". There are a variety of ways or "ministries" that are available to us. You will feel drawn to at least one of them. It usually begins with worshipping God. As we sing praises to our Heavenly Father, we connect with Him. Then He begins to reveal the talents that He has already given to you. The friends you make at church will confirm that for you. You are equipped to handle a particular ministry. To give some examples: you can play an instrument or sing, you're comfortable speaking to people about what you have learned, you enjoy visiting people, you like to teach kids about Jesus, you're good at repairing things, you're good at comforting people who are going through something that you have already experienced – such as divorce or single parenting, you have an ability to organize fund raisers or charities, you can operate technical equipment, even serving coffee at church is a ministry. It provides a service for your teammates. In the eyes of Jesus, that ministry is no less valuable than a ministry of evangelism where a person is preaching about Jesus on a missions trip. Why? Because none of us actually has a personal ministry. We all participate in the ministry of Jesus. All of His ministries are of equal importance.

When you associate with Christians, hang out with the ones who know Jesus in the same way as you. They recognize the intimacy that we have in the Lord. Avoid the ones who would compromise your relationship with Jesus. For example, some churched people told a new Christian that God was not a puppet to act on your every prayer. Again, a pastor told his church that "we shouldn't pester the Deity with prayers". Ridiculous. Listen to that Teacher inside you – the Holy Spirit. He will tell you that they are wrong, but love them anyway. Please don't argue. Even though they can't see the truth that has been revealed to you, they are still part of the family. You may voice your concern, but only in a loving way, not a forceful way. They may be corrected but only in God's timing and only when they choose to change.

CHAPTER SIX

To Venture Forth

An evangelist once said that Jesus came to change people. Now that we have been changed, He can move through us to continue to change people. What an honour it is to become an ambassador for Jesus. Our willingness to share our faith does not come from a sense of duty. It's an expression of joy and of love as we reflect Jesus to the people around us. Even though you have been lit up inside, you are entering an arena that has been damaged. This is the area where people push their religion onto you.

We need to be non-aggressive, leave Jesus in control in this arena. He will set you up with an opportunity to speak. Maybe a friend is having difficulty in his life and is sharing the problem with you. Maybe someone starts talking about religion. In any case, you will recognize the opportunity to say something. Wait for a moment before you say something to allow Jesus to speak to your heart. This is His domain and He promises to lead you: "For it is not you who speak, but it is the Spirit of your Father who speaks in you" [Matthew 10:20]. That second of surrender opens the door for the Holy Spirit to speak through you. He may prompt you to say something you had never thought of before; or to share how He changed your life. Whatever you say will touch the heart of the person with whom you are talking, because these words are coming from God Himself. Do not look for a pattern or a specific way to talk to people. Everyone is unique and God's response will be unique to that person. Do not let your mind override the words that Jesus is putting into your heart, or you will be putting your words into God's mouth.

If a person starts to argue with you, back off. What you have already said is enough to remain in that person's heart. Our words are not meant to deal with the rationale of the mind. They are meant to bring life to the heart. Don't be discouraged or offended if someone does not accept what you are saying. That person is not accepting what Jesus is saying. Accepting or not, Jesus has put a seed into that heart. You don't need to see it sprout.

On the flip side, someone has seen the change in your life and would like prayer to receive Jesus. How do you pray for this person? Very simply, all the person has to do is to ask Jesus into his or her heart. The order of words doesn't matter. In fact, people can do this on their own. For the most part, a person feels more comfortable repeating a prayer after you. I like to take the person by the hand as he or she repeats this prayer: Heavenly Father, forgive me for the things I have done wrong. I ask the Lord Jesus to come into my heart now, and to create a new life within me. I pray in Your Name Jesus, Amen. Again, the wording doesn't matter. Jesus will respond to a willing heart, period.

So someone else comes to you for prayer – nothing specific. Now how do you pray? Easy, the Holy Spirit does the praying for you. I like to ask the person if I may put my hand on the shoulder. There is a good reason for that. The Holy Spirit lives inside of you. It is the most powerful force in the world because it comes from outside of this world. As you pray for that person that force transfers into the person's body. It has the potential to deliver this person from demonic forces, to heal sickness and disease, to transform both the heart and the mind and to bestow a peace that never leaves. You don't need to know what's going to happen, or even what to pray for. You start by praising God because we are so grateful to participate with Him. Then ask the Holy Spirit to touch this person. Then the prayer language takes over. Remember how you learned a new way of praying called speaking in tongues? Just start speaking the words that the Holy Spirit is giving to you. It doesn't matter if you can only say a few words. Just repeat them over and over again. Those words are Spirit led and break into the spiritual realm. Don't stop praying until the person indicates that Jesus has completed His ministry on him or her. I have seen people stand motionless anywhere from 3 minutes to 3 hours. Don't ask what happened. That is a personal issue between the person and Jesus.

Finally, if you make a mistake, don't lose heart. The enemy will stab you with a needle of fear. Instead, remember this picture. Imagine yourself picking up a rock and placing it on the ground in front of you. That rock represents your mistake. Now imagine a rock cliff behind your rock. As you look up, this cliff extends so high you can't see the top of it. This cliff represents the love that Jesus has for you. Which one is bigger? Your rock is insignificant, and it doesn't matter. Now imagine picking up your rock and throwing it away. Then walk to the rock cliff, turn around and sit on the ground. Now lean back so your back is resting on this cliff. The love of Jesus has your back. Listen to Him who will bring about something good from something bad. [Romans 8:28]. He will show you the right thing to do.

This is all you need to know. Don't complicate the simplicity of praying for people. Jesus would love to have

CHAPTER SEVEN

Topics of Interest

APPLICATION – Sometimes the heart can be very defensive around small things that prevent us from becoming more like Jesus. It's human nature since we are not perfect. Once we identify those things we search the Bible for a spiritual truth that will deal with them. Apply that truth, or that verse, to your life. Don't give up. Persist in applying that truth and it will overcome those obstacles. It will bring life to a lifeless area in your heart. If you give up the Holy Spirit will convict you [not condemn you] time and again. The Lord does not want you to miss out on the joy that he has for you. The more you apply the truths of the Bible to your life, the more you will see God at work in your life.

BAPTISM – Baptism is a public celebration of your commitment to Jesus. Going underwater is symbolic of getting buried as Jesus was. Coming up out of the water symbolizes getting raised from the dead just like Jesus. It is an affirmation of God's promise to cleanse us from all wrongdoing and to guarantee a place for us in Heaven.

BRIDE – You may hear the phrase "Bride of Christ". This refers to the church, which is us, not the building.

We are spiritually united with Jesus. This phrase is usually associated with other terms like "second coming" or "rapture". These terms signify the return of Jesus [spiritually speaking, not physical] who will take us to our home in Heaven. How this is to play out is not important. Academic debate will mess with your head and cause harm to your faith. His sacrifice has made us pure and worthy to enter Heaven. Do not say that you are not worthy because that will negate His sacrifice, which tells Him that He died for nothing. Our simple faith allows His righteousness to go before us. Our faults and our failures will be left behind when we enter Heaven.

CHOICE- If you tell God what is best for you then you really don't care about Him. Choose to let Him show you what is best for you. With every decision you make, open your heart first and expect an answer from God. I hear an audible voice now, but it didn't start out that way. It started with impressions on the heart. You will receive a discernment where you feel the distinction between the right choice and the wrong choice. As you grow in your relationship with Jesus you will hear His voice in your heart.

COMMITMENT – A commitment, by definition, is a pledge or a promise to do something in the future. We are 100% committed to Jesus for the rest of our lives. He said, "Seek first His kingdom and His righteousness; and all these things shall be added to you." [Matthew 6:33]. The kingdom is the supernatural realm which coexists with the natural realm. Righteousness involves our moral conduct with other people. The providence of God will be added to us because His kingdom works for us. A Jewish man repaired a car engine. When it started he spoke the Hebrew word for righteous. The motor was operating perfectly as it was designed to do. So the kingdom works for us when we put Jesus first in our lives.

CONFESSION – If there is one area of weakness in a Christian life, it is confession. It was a standard in the Early Church: "Therefore confess your sins to each other and pray for each other, so that you may be healed. The prayer of a righteous person is powerful and effective". [James 5:16]. Today we don't want to air our dirty laundry unless we have a good friend we can trust. If we don't feel comfortable with anyone, then we can confess to God on our own.

DISCERNMENT – The spirit of discernment is a great weapon of protection. The Holy Spirit has given you this gift and it acts like a holy filter. It allows you to recognize what is true and what is false. We will be subjected to false teachings because human nature is corruptible. God has given us an incorruptible spirit that can identify them for you. Listen with your heart and you will be shown the right path.

DISCIPLINE – Discipline means training. It keeps us on the rails as we listen to what the Holy Spirit is saying to us. It's the path to becoming more like Jesus. It involves reading the NEW TESTAMENT, communing with your Heavenly Father through prayer, worshipping God in the church service and participating in a bible study with other Christians. These are not rules. They are responses to what God has given to us and we need to be responsible for our behaviour. What you learn from these responses will align with what the Holy Spirit is teaching you internally. You will become Christ-centered instead of self-centered. It's no longer about you, it's about Jesus.

DISTINCTION – What makes us distinct, or different, from other people is our recognition of inner beauty. Whenever inner beauty is omitted in any life, every other thing around that life, no matter how beautiful, will be affected. Agents of decay will be sent to attack them. Physical beauty, created by God, has been given to the world. It has a way of introducing idolatry [loving something more than God]. Inner beauty is heavenly and is precious in God's sight. It manifests itself in holiness. The grace of God [unmerited favour of God] will produce holy character, behaviour and service in spite of our sinful nature. God who is holy will produce in us holy thoughts, holy living and pure motives. We become holy in heart because of His Holy Spirit. We become stronger in our actions as His righteousness is given to us. We shine from the inside out. Jesus expects you not to hide it as He says, "Let your light so shine before men that they may see your good works and glorify your Father in Heaven". [Matthew 5:16].

EMPOWERMENT – Since you met Jesus His love continues to fill your heart. You want to do something for Him. He is not going to leave you on your own to do it. That divine love contains all the miraculous powers from our Creator. We don't need to convince people, we just have to pray for them. St. Paul, who wrote more than 25% of the New Testament, says, "My message and my preaching were not in persuasive words of wisdom, but in demonstration of the Spirit and of power, that your faith should not rest on the wisdom of men, but on the power of God." [I Corinthians 2:4,5]. We don't even have to ask what to pray for. When you lay your hand on someone and pray in tongues, the Lord releases His power through you to change a life in a miraculous way. Jesus wants you to stand in His place. How cool is that?

EXAMPLE – Our lifestyle is our testimony of God living inside of us. Jesus told us a parable of the Good Samaritan. I would like to give you a modern day example of that. When I was in Ireland I saw a drunk man who had fallen down. He was bleeding from a head wound. I got a clean wet cloth from a nearby corner store and wiped his wound clean. Then I bought a band-aid from a health store and covered the wound. Then I bought him some food and a drink. With tears in his eyes, he said no one has ever cared for him like that except for his Mother. Later two Christians stopped me to say that they had seen my compassion on that man and they were in shock. Yet this is how we are supposed to act. Jesus told us that the way we behave towards those who are less fortunate reflects the way we behave towards Him.

FORGIVENESS – Forgiveness is the single most important attribute to obtain in your life. It is almost impossible to completely forgive on your own. Retaliation is in our nature, forgiveness is from divine nature. It comes down to a choice. We have to choose to let the Holy Spirit put His forgiveness into our hearts. Don't be discouraged if it takes some time. It took me ten years of praying every day before I could forgive the man who sexually abused me as a child. It was worth it. There are no scars on my heart. It is as if it never happened. Our service in the ministry of Jesus will be limited until we can forgive completely.

MATURITY – Sometimes the power that you have been given is ready for an increase, but your character isn't ready. Be keenly aware of your motives. Don't let this power lure you into selfish gain. It is meant for the people around you. When His power confronts crime, forgiveness happens;

when it collides with disease, people are healed; when it runs into demonized people, they are set free. The purpose of this power is to glorify God. Listen before you act. The motive is not based on the ministry, it's based on glorifying God. Maturity is also needed when it comes to giving away money. If someone comes to you for prayer, and then asks for money afterwards, the answer is no – unless the Lord tells you otherwise. Don't enable a wrong motive. We pray for matters of the heart.

REDEMPTION – This is a foundational word in the church. Simply put, it means a restoration of a broken relationship. Anything evil has to be abolished before we can enter Heaven where evil does not exist. Jesus, the divine Son of God, took that evil upon Himself and allowed Himself to be murdered as a blood sacrifice to abolish the evil. Now we can enter Heaven free from "sin." Jesus restored the relationship between man and God, He redeemed us from a life of separation.

RELIANCE – To be totally reliant on God, you must take other desires out of your heart and focus 100% on what God is asking of you. When you set your heart right before God, then the mind will find the right things to look for. Then you can rely on Him to provide them.

RIDICULE – It hurts when someone makes fun of you. If someone laughs at you because of your faith, just pray for that person. That person is still valuable to Jesus and your prayer will help. Keep this promise in your heart: "If you are reviled for the name of Christ, you are blessed, because the Spirit of glory and of God rests upon you." [I Peter 4:14].

SALVATION – Salvation is the heart and soul of the Christian faith. It is no longer a life and death world, it is a life and new life world. The resurrection of Jesus from the dead is our guarantee. St. Paul says, "If you confess with your mouth Jesus as Lord, and believe in your heart that God raised Him from the dead, you shall be saved." [Romans 10:9] These words were written in an ancient Greek language. That Greek word SAVED can be expressed in three tenses. When we met Jesus, as we live with Jesus, and when we enter Heaven with Jesus, are all described as saved. So past, present and future are embodied in our faith. Salvation is complete in itself.

SELF-CONTROL – There is a list of character traits that are given to us when we meet Jesus. We acquire these traits as the Holy Spirit releases them into our hearts. They are: love, joy, peace, patience, kindness, goodness, faithfulness, gentleness and self-control [Galatians 5: 22,23]. The last one, self-control, is the hardest one to assimilate, or take in. The others involve the emotions; self-control involves both the emotions and the mind. We must actively take hold of this gift when we face unhealthy thoughts and allow it to rule over any subsequent behaviour. Your actions will then be under grace which comes from God.

STRUCTURE – Each one of us is a valuable ambassador of love. Most of us are comfortable in our own skin to talk about Jesus. Others want to talk about Jesus but are not so comfortable. They need some sort of structure, or guidelines to follow. I was an exceedingly shy little girl so I can relate to that. During my three years of world travel, the Lord granted me insights on how to evangelize. For those of you who would like a place of structure, here are my pointers:

1. In your mind, let the person become a family member to you, or a close friend.
2. Open your heart to the Holy Spirit and let Him guide you.
3. Be a good listener, don't speak too quickly.
4. Be patient, you care enough to spend time with this person.
5. If a person becomes quarrelsome, do not argue. Respectfully excuse yourself if you are facing abuse. You are not required to listen to slander.
6. Follow through by contacting that person later.
7. If someone confides in you, don't tell anyone. Keep it confidential and offer to pray for that person.

TRADITION – A tradition is a belief or behaviour that is passed down from generation to generation, a custom that originated in the past. One such tradition that is celebrated in the Christian faith is called Communion. When Jesus ate His last meal with His disciples, He asked them to remember Him as He gave them both bread and wine. We celebrate this tradition today because it was initiated by Jesus. The bread represents His body that would be sacrificed for our wrongdoings. The wine represents His blood that would signify a new promise for mankind that will guarantee our place in Heaven.

We can celebrate this tradition in the church service or outside of the church. We can celebrate our communion with Jesus at any time.

The Key

Wondering what has happened to you and what you are to do next is a natural response when the Holy Spirit has touched your heart. The key is to choose to deepen your love for Jesus. That CHOICE opens the door for your new journey with Him.

Final Note

Marlena's first book MAY I PRAY FOR YOU is a testimonial of praying for people as she travelled around the world.

This is her second book, designed as a handbook, for new believers in Jesus Christ. The purpose is to help these people move forward in their Christian lives.

Epilogue

To understand the nature of this ministry of Jesus, I would like to summarize from my first book which is called May I Pray For You? The summary will include my background, the call to serve and the effect the Holy Spirit had on the people for whom I prayed.

The background - My journey with Jesus started at the age of four. My dad led me in a prayer to invite Jesus into my heart. This was significant because at the age of five I was sexually abused by a family friend. This abuse continued for five years. During this time I held on to Jesus because I knew He loved me and no one else seemed to care. Actually, no one knew about the abuse. During the following five years I fell deeper and deeper into depression. At the age of fifteen I exploded with rage and ended up as a drug addicted prostitute for three years. Then one evening, while I was in a "crack shack", the Holy Spirit broke into the building. It was as if a veil had been lifted from my eyes and I could see all the harm I was causing to myself and to others. It was so overwhelming that I ran from the building and continued to run for five miles until I arrived at my parent's home. To my surprise my parents were waiting for me. My Mother placed an elegant white robe around me and said. "This is the righteousness of Jesus Christ." How did they know that

I was coming home? It turns out that my parents, who had been praying for me for three years, had been approached by two old friends who wanted to pray with them for forty days, specifically for the Holy Spirit to touch me. The four of them met every morning at 5:30 and prayed for me for an hour. On the fortieth day, the Lord spoke to my Mother and said that I would be coming home that night. She bought the robe on that day. I was sick for two weeks as my body was in "detox" mode. Then I felt clean, and I began a thirteen year journey of loving Jesus. I attended church and bible studies. I wanted people to pray for me and I asked Jesus to heal me in every area. I knew that my heart had been damaged, but He healed it completely, even to the point where I could forgive the man who had abused me. I wanted to do something for Him.

The call to serve - I had heard the Lord's voice as impressions on my heart for thirteen years. Then, in 2013, He started to speak audibly to me. He called me to pray for people in three countries. The first country was Belize where He put me on national television as I shared my testimony. The second country was Costa Rica where people were so touched by the Holy Spirit that they could not remain standing. They fell backward as the Holy Spirit overpowered them. I began to sing to the Lord every morning and every evening, a devotion that continues to this day. The third country was Spain. The only church I could find was in a commercial building where the people were too timid to share Jesus. In fact, the sermon was on how to defend yourself when someone discovers that you are a Christian. When I went back to the hotel I asked Jesus why He had asked me to come here. That is when He told me to make a sign that reads "May I Pray For You" and to stand with it in a busy place. This time people were physically healed as I prayed for them. When I returned home I asked Jesus, "What more can I do for You?" He said, "I want you to go to Brazil, one way." I was shocked, and said, "One way?" He told me to give up everything and He would take me around the world over the next two years. I told Him that I loved Him more than anything else in this world and I will do anything for Him. I gave away my possessions, shut down my facebook, cancelled my life insurance and gave my sister power of attorney to handle my taxes. On September 15, 2015, I flew one way to Rio de Janeiro.

The effect of the Holy Spirit - When I arrived in Rio, I found a supply store where I purchased a steel framed whiteboard sign. Someone at my hostel showed me how to write "May I pray for you?" in Portuguese. The next day I walked to a busy plaza and stood beside a monument. I rested the sign against my knees and waited. Within one minute a lady approached me to receive prayer. I told her I could pray only in English. She smiled and answered me in Portuguese and I heard the word that sounded like "universal." I put my hand on her shoulder and as I prayed in English I could feel the Holy Spirit prompting me to speak "in tongues" which is a prayer that had been given to me. She stood motionless for ten minutes. She spoke softly several times as if she were conversing with Jesus. Then she took a deep breath and opened her eyes. She hugged me and spoke to me in Portuguese, which I didn't understand. The same thing happened to the next two people who came to me for prayer. Then I prayed for a person who spoke English. After ten minutes she also took a deep breath and opened her eyes. She said she had a personal conversation with Jesus and He had healed her heart. She said she breathed in the Holy Spirit and received a peace in her heart that she had never experienced before. All four of these people had a brightness in their eyes and seemed full of joy. With each day, more and more people came for prayer, all standing motionless as they encountered Jesus. I was asked to speak in a church that was so grateful they gave me money so I could travel to Sao Paulo. The same thing happened when I stood with the sign on a busy plaza. After receiving prayer, one man would grab people off the street saying, "You've got to get prayer from her!" Jesus continued to touch people in this manner as He took me around the world for the next two years. I would not take money from people when they came to me for prayer. It was the churches and some business people who gave me money so I could continue around the world. They have a huge part in this ministry of Jesus. These are the countries where I stood with the sign:

Brazil
Argentina
Peru
Ecuador
Columbia
Uganda
Kenya
Ethiopia
Ireland
Poland
Romania
Macedonia
New Zealand
Australia
Indonesia
Malaysia
Philippines
China [Hong Kong]

Taiwan
South Korea
Japan
Canada

Even though I had packed a sleeping bag because I thought I would be sleeping outside, the Lord Jesus gave me a roof over my head every single day on this journey. I had enough food every day and did not lack anything. When Jesus calls you to serve Him, He will look after you as He equips you. We serve an amazing God. Bless Him forever, Marlena.

My thanks to WestBow Press and the wonderful people who helped me with this book.